I0181480

31 Days Of Instant Inspiration

"Be Inspired"

ANDREA FREEMAN

Copyright ©2014 Andrea Freeman

All Rights Reserved. No part of this book may be reproduced or transmitted in any form or by any means, electronic or mechanical, including photocopying, recording, or by any information storage and retrieval system, without prior written permission from the Author/Publisher of this book, except for the inclusion of brief quotations in printed reviews.

Scriptures taken from New International Version Bible

ISBN: 978-0-615-97817-8 Published in U.S. by Changing Lives And Sincerely Supporting You, Inc.

Contents

Day One

Instant Inspiration of **Thankfulness**

Today, I am so **thankful** for God's provision; that all of my needs are met according to His riches in glory; and that I may prosper in all areas of my life as my soul shall prosper. I am **thankful** in advance that my latter days shall be greater than my former.

"Rejoice always, pray continually, give **thanks** in all circumstances; for this is God's will for you in Christ Jesus."

1Thessalonians 5:16-18

Thankfulness

We should be thankful because God is worthy of our thanksgiving. When we are thankful our focus moves away from selfish desires and the pain of our current circumstances. Expressing thankfulness helps us to remember that God is in control. It reminds us of the bigger picture; that we belong to God.

Sometimes, being thankful is hard when you are faced with divorce, depression, being overwhelmed, and other issues but God wants us to be thankful even in our difficult times. That's an act of faith, and God is always working beyond our circumstances. We should always have gratitude regardless of the type of circumstances we have.

It's always easier to be thankful when "All is well." We should not just praise God in the moment, but remember His past faithfulness. Thankfulness should be a way of life for us and should naturally come from the heart. Do you realize how much you have been given?

We should be thankful for waking up because there is someone who didn't. We should be thankful for vision because there is someone who cannot see. We should be thankful for ALL things, whether great or small.

Day Two

Instant Inspiration of **Faithfulness**

Today, I will make God's **faithfulness** known everywhere I go because I trust His word. I believe that God will fulfill His promises and I will stay in a close walk with Him, with a **faithful** heart.

"I will sing of the Lord's great love forever; with my mouth I will make your **faithfulness** known through all generations." *Psalm 89:1*

Faithfulness

How many times have you promised your small child that you would do something but it slipped your mind? With so many things to balance in life, you may have unintentionally forgot and suddenly your child is deeply disappointed.

Although we live in a world of broken promises, God doesn't forget His promises because He is faithful. We should be glad that God's faithfulness says, "I will honor My Word." When we trust and believe God, our faith is being strengthened and our eternal destiny is secure. Even when our faith fails, God's faithfulness never will because faithfulness is an attribute of God. Have there been times when you've applied everything that you learned and it didn't work? Have there been times when you've tried everything that you can to get the door open and it never opened? But God remained faithful and opened doors that no man could shut.

Think about all of the times that you have created a huge mess in your own life. You have been faced with numerous challenges and were unable to figure out how you would overcome. Although God had absolutely nothing to do with them, He has allowed them to happen because we do have free will. He has no desire to see us endure pain and has always provided a way out.

Trust God and have faith because the solution is beyond you. God will −always− keep you in the midst of your calamities.

Day Three

Instant Inspiration of **Love**

Today, I will choose to **love** every person (regardless of who they are), just as God loved me. I will not be self-seeking or bear grudges but obey His commands. I recognized that God is the source of all of our **love** and that we **love** because He loved us first.

"As the Father has **loved** me, so have I **loved** you. Now remain in My **love**. If you keep My commands, you will remain in my **love**, just as I have kept my Father's commands and remain in His **love**. I have told you this is so that My joy may be in you and that your joy may be complete. My command is this: **Love** each other as I have **loved** you."
John 15:9-12

Love

Have you ever loved someone so much that you can't seem to control your feelings for them? Often, it's people who have grown on us or become really close to us. For instance, our children, parents, spouse, etc. They have made us feel like our entire worlds have changed for the better. Life appears to be so beautiful and we couldn't imagine living without them.

We love the person without limitations and our love appears to be excessive. Suddenly, that person fails us and although we are deeply hurt, we still show unconditional love for them.

They have hurt us over and over again but we continue to show love; allowing them to reside in a special place...OUR HEARTS! Although they hurt us more than the enemy we CHOOSE to love them.

Let's make a choice to love everyone. Love is one of God's most important commandments and for some reason we only seem to "self-select" whom we will love.

If someone talks about us, we hate them. If the neighbor takes our parking space, we stop speaking to them. This behavior is not pleasing to God. God commands us to love our enemies and do good to those who hate us. Even if we don't agree, God commands us to love our neighbors as ourselves.

We demonstrate our love for God by obeying His commandments. Let your attitude of love, consideration, and compassion for others prove your love for God.

Day Four

Instant Inspiration of **Peace**

Today, I will find **peace** by keeping my mind and thoughts focused on Him. If I make contact and stay connected to Him, I know that He will keep me covered under His feathers and wings. I have the presence of the Lord, who gives me **PEACE!**

"**Peace** I leave you; my **peace** I give you. I do not give you as the world gives. Do not let your hearts be troubled and do not be afraid."
John 14:27

Peace

Sometimes you sit and think, *"All I want is peace."* You have humbled yourself but you still can't seem to find peace. You wonder, *"Why can't I just live in peace?"* It's because you are tying to manufacture your own peace in the natural. Unfortunately, that will never happen.

It doesn't make sense for a person to be in trouble in the natural, and expect to be at rest in peace while they are in trouble. Peace will be found by making contact with the person and presence of Jesus. Peace is found by making contact with the presence of His word.

When you are going through some type of fiery furnace, you need Jesus peace. That is a peace that passes all understanding and leaves you victorious regardless of what your circumstances are. You won't have to worry about anything because Jesus has already covered it.

When you need a shield from the fiery darts thrown by the enemy, His truth will be your shield and buckler. Just train your mind and thoughts to stay with Jesus. Keep your mind on Him and you will find yourself in perfect peace.

You can cry to the Lord for His unmerited favor and there is a refuge or a safe hiding place that you can go until the storm passes. You will be protected from the winds and the rain because of the supernatural Jesus peace, that will turn that turmoil into peace. Jesus peace is your strength because He can touch what you are feeling inside.

Day Five

Instant Inspiration of **Happiness**

Today, I will be in pursuit of **happiness** regardless of my circumstances. Life and it's many distractions will not grab my attention. I claim that **happiness** shall follow me all the days of my life.

"I know that there is nothing better for people than to be **happy** and to do good while they live. That each of them may eat and drink, and find satisfaction in all their toil- this is the gift of God."

Ecclesiastes 3:12-13

Happiness

Often, it feels as if your happiness is somehow related to your circumstances. If your circumstances are good you are happy. If your circumstances are bad you are not happy. Truthfully, happiness has absolutely nothing to do with your circumstances. Happiness is a choice and the result of the choice. God is your Lord. You should feel extremely blessed. Rejoice in the Lord always.

What you focus on and the perspective you embrace concerning your circumstances will determine your happiness. God will use your circumstances for His purposes and your good. Lay back and enjoy your voyage, because God is your strong tower and He will protect you. He is your friend and He will never leave your side. Focus your feelings and sense of well-being on the things that you cannot see in this world, rather than the things you can see (your circumstances). If you can control your perspective you can control your happiness. Follow the voice of God by faith and it will drive your behavior, attitude, and happiness.

You may not be able to change your circumstances but God can. Smile and be content with wherever you are and whatever you have. Count your blessings and don't run to substitutes. Run to God, be obedient, and follow His commandments.

The higher your positive energy, the higher the state of your spirituality and happiness. Smile and BE HAPPY!

Day Six

Instant Inspiration of **Hope**

Today, I will be filled with **hope**. Regardless of my circumstances, I know that God plans to give me **hope** and I will remain **hopeful** until I see the promise come to pass. I will submit myself to God because He is the source of my **hope**. Although I cannot see how God is perfecting me, I will rejoice in the Lord!

"But those who **hope** in the Lord will renew their strength. They will soar on wings like eagles; they will run and not grow weary, they will walk and not be faint." *Isaiah 40:31*

Hope

As the song says, "My hope is built on nothing less than Jesus' blood and righteousness." Your hope should be in the Lord and He will fill you with joy and peace.

Sometimes, you may not understand but you must have hope. Sometimes, you may not see how it will come to pass but you must have hope. Your hope is your strength and you shall wait with patience.

Yes, times are hard and you are uncertain of what your future holds but God knows your future and you must put your hope in His word. Be confident that He is your anchor in the present and for the future. Trust that He will rescue you while you are in the storm.

You may not be rich but God has secured you. His promises are for tomorrow, next week, next year, and forever. The Lord is delighted when you put your hope in Him and His unfailing love. He wants you to depend on Him for everything, and you need not be ashamed.

God loves you and you are the apple of His eye. You cannot fully hope with 100% certainty that your job, inheritance, or retirement fund will protect you but you must know that God will.

You can no longer wrestle with what will happen tomorrow because with hope in God, you can find rest. His promises are rock-solid. Do you realize that He has already taken care of you?

Day Seven

Instant Inspiration of **Favor**

Today, I claim accelerated **favor**. I know that God is working things out for my own good. What should take me a lifetime to accomplish, will not take me ten years, or even ten months because God will give me preferential treatment. I will win battles that I didn't even have to fight.

"And God is able to bless you abundantly, so that in all things at all times, having all that you need, you will abound in every good work."

2Corinthians 9:8

Favor

Life is difficult and sometimes feels as if it may be one of the most trying times any person could ever endure. It seems the harder you try, the harder you fall. The more you work, the more you need.

In the midst of your darkest hour and all of your pain, you must know that the favor of the Lord will be upon you. He is the strength of your life and your difficult situation will turn around. Your inheritance has been predestined and God has positioned you to receive divine favor.

You may be tired and even feel beaten, but God is preparing to advance you. You are gaining speed and you shall not look back. Regardless of your circumstances, you must boldly declare that *God's favor is coming your way.*

Just when it seems as if your boat is sinking and you are helpless, your life jacket −God− somehow seems to save you. Therefore, you must keep on believing, expecting, and declaring God's favor over your life.

You cannot go around and complain about being in debt. You cannot complain about being mistreated by people. You cannot complain about being at a disadvantage. God has already placed you at an advantage and you must have an attitude of faith. Be on the look out for God's goodness.

Yes, you have made many mistakes and have done a lot of wrong things but know that God's goodness is going to show up in your life in a new way.

Day Eight

Instant Inspiration of **Grace**

Today, I am grateful for God's **grace**. Although I am a sinner, He continues to bestow **grace** upon me. God provides a sustaining **grace** in the season of my pain. He has an inexhaustible reservoir of resources that can never be diminished. For His **grace** is sufficient.

"Three times I pleaded with the Lord to take it away from me. But He said to me, 'My **grace** is sufficient for you, for my power is mad perfect in weakness.' Therefore, I will boast all the more gladly about my weakness, so that Christ's power may rest on me."
2Corinthians 12:8-9

Grace

God is rich in grace and He gives us grace that we absolutely don't deserve. Often we say we believe in God and He is our father but we do not always live up to truly honoring and obeying Him. God constantly bestows His grace upon us. As sinners, He wakes us up in the mornings, allows us to have food, shelter, and clothing. God gives everyone that grace.

What's even more amazing is the fact that when we truly commit to God, the work of the Holy Spirit can effectively move and cause internal and external transformation. That qualifies us to be recipients of God and receive the full benefits of Him.

Our sins are forgiven and God will provide us an abundance of blessings.

He will provide sufficient and sustaining grace in the season of our pain. God will provide healing, comfort, and assurance. There will be no mountain too high to climb, no valley too low to cross, and no pain, suffering, or burdens that we cannot bear.

Thank God for His grace that guides your purpose, stirs your compassion, and frees your mind. Through awareness and understanding, you shall not feel angry, frustrated, sad, helpless, or depressed. With God's grace, He has liberated you from those emotions that attempt to enslave you.

Day Nine

Instant Inspiration of **Blessings**

Today, I will praise God from whom all **blessings** flow. I recognize that my very life is a **blessing**. I will have a heart of gratitude and forget not all His benefits. He has satisfied me and if He never **blesses** me another day in life, I will continue to give Him all of the glory.

"**Blessed** is the one who perseveres under trial because, having stood the test, that person will receive the crown of life that the Lord has promised to those who love Him." *James 1:12*

Blessings

It is time for the blessings of God to run after His people. You need not feel defeated or frustrated trying to get what God has already promised you. God says, that he will –command– His blessings to come upon you. They shall run after and overtake you. God has promised you His blessings and supernatural provision.

In the 28th chapter of Deuteronomy, we can see God's purpose to bless and prosper His people being clearly revealed. It is time for God's blessing to be released into your life and nothing can stop it.

Claim your blessing. Tell yourself that you know God doesn't want you to worry about bills or barely surviving. God plans to prosper you and to meet all of your needs but you must have faith. Don't be bound to the pressures of life because God wants His blessings to continually flow into your life. Expect God's blessings to be poured upon you. Claim prosperity and increase, so that your needs are met.

It's great to praise God when you receive big blessings but it's even more important that you thank Him for the small things. Thank God for your vision to read this book. Thank God for your hearing. Thank God for −ALL THINGS− because you are blessed.

His Word says that you will be blessed in the city and in the field. His words says that you will be blessed when you come and when you go. Act in faith and obedience, so that you can see the fulfillment of God's promises.

Day Ten

Instant Inspiration of **Victory**

Today, **Victory** is "MINE." Satan can continue to wander about seeking those whom he may devour, but his works are destroyed. I will not be taken by the lies of satan or his temptations. I will follow what God says, because His Word will not fail me. I will walk in **VICTORY!**

"But thanks be to God! He gives us the **victory** through our Lord, Jesus Christ." *1 Corinthians 15:57*

Victory

When you think about victory you think about winning. When you think about winning sometimes you think about a race. Christianity can be difficult, so you must prepare to be in a race of faith in order to be victorious. Preparation requires you to pray, read the bible, and practice other day to day biblical principles. It prepares your faith to endure and helps prevent you from being disqualified.

God wants you to keep running and His strength will sustain you. He wants to reward you for a strong finish but you must understand that satan will try and pull you back into an old life of sin. You will be in a spiritual battle or in spiritual warfare and satan will try and destroy you. When he sees you honoring and obeying God and receiving blessings he is going to send every attack possible on you.

In times of difficulty, guard your mind and press on toward the goal to be victorious. Forget what lies behind and push forward. Remain steadfast in faith and you will see the fulfillment of God's promises.

Please keep in mind that although satan and life in general will present many occasions that will tempt you to doubt God or give up. God's goal for every Christian is VICTORY! He has provided heavenly resources that enable us to do His will. There will be a day of reward for those who persevere.

Day Eleven

Instant Inspiration of **Increase**

Today, I claim **increase** in my income. I claim **increase** in my strength. I claim **increase** in my wisdom. I claim that wherever I am lacking God will **increase**. He will make all grace abound toward me and pour out so many blessings that I will not have enough room for them.

"Now he who supplies seed to the sower and bread for food will also supply and **increase** your store of seed and will enlarge the harvest of your righteousness." *2 Corinthians 9:10*

Increase

God promised "Ye shall eat the increase." God's blessings will be commanded upon every area of your life. He promises a land flowing with milk and honey. Therefore, you must not forget that it was God who supernaturally increased and prospered you. Never forget God and mistakenly think that you were increased on your own. God's strength, wisdom, and abilities is what helped you acquire all that you have.

God is your Source of supply so remember to always give God your best. Everything you do should be done *to the glory of God.* Wake up in the morning saying, "I will make my bed to the glory of God. I will go to work to the glory of God. I will be productive to the glory of God." Trust God to meet all of your needs.

Giving to God's work is an investment with eternal rewards for you. It stores up treasures in heaven for you. Jesus promises that if we sacrifice now, the return on our investment will be a hundredfold in eternity. Make God's work a priority.

Continually praise God for the divine favor that is in your life. Praise Him for His goodness, mercy, and grace and expect and believe that God is going to manifest everyday in your life. This is your season of increase!

Day Twelve

Instant Inspiration of **Trust**

Today, I will place all of my **trust** in my Heavenly Father. I will walk the way God wants me to walk even if there is no reward. I believe that I have more than access to God. I also have a standing invitation into His very presence. I −**TRUST**− in the Lord with all my heart.

"When I am afraid, I will **trust** in you. In God, whose word I praise, in God I **trust**; I will not be afraid. What can mortal man do to me?" *Psalm 56:3-4*

Trust

Throughout life we have all faced challenges with trust. Many of us can recall growing up telling our best friends a secret that would end up in everyone else's ears within minutes. Although they could never seem to keep a secret we would go back and tell them more secrets, over and over again. Finally, we lost the trust we had and had a hard time trusting anyone.

Many of us have developed wrong attitudes and have allowed trust issues with people to keep us from trusting God as well. The bible says to "Trust in the −LORD− with all thine heart." God is not man and He can always be trusted. His ways are not our ways and His thoughts are not our thoughts. He desires and requires that we trust Him at all times.

When you trust God you have peace with Him through our Lord Jesus Christ. We have a standing invitation to the very presence and throne room of God. It's a great feeling to know that if we just trust Him, He will direct our paths, and make them straight.

Even in our darkest hours we should be of good cheer. We shall not fear or be afraid because God will grant us grace and mercy, even during a catastrophe. He is Jehovah-Nissi, our banner of love and protection!

Day Thirteen

Instant Inspiration of **Abundant Life**

Today, I believe that God wants me to live an **abundant** life. If I will obey, He will give me happiness in it's fullest measure. God will give me a peace that surpasses ALL understanding. I have access to Him and the privilege of entering into His presence through the work of Jesus Christ. I will rejoice!

"The thief cometh not, but for to steal, and to kill, and to destroy: I am come that they might have life, and that they might have it more **abundantly**." *John 10:10*

Abundant Life

With so much going on in the world today, it is hard for many to feel like they are living anything close to an abundant life. With the rising costs of gas, food, and shelter and employee layoffs it almost seems impossible.

Many feel as if there is *too much month and too little money*. Some even feel depressed, unhappy, frustrated, hopeless, and empty and look for escape routes such as self-pity, drugs, alcohol or even suicide.

Those feelings are not how God wants us to feel. He wants His joy to remain you. He desires to place you on a path to enjoying a wonderful, abundant life. He says, "Your sorrow shall be turned into joy and no man can take this joy from you." God wants you to trust Him doing times of trial and suffering. Sometimes we don't understand but we must have the presence of God's spirit within our minds, so we can experience peace even when we are being persecuted. When we have peace we can rejoice in our sufferings and God's glory shall be revealed. If we endure until the end, there will be a glorious reward that awaits us.

Count it all joy and be strong in the Lord and you will defeat enemies and conquer fear. You will have wisdom, knowledge and understanding; which will drive the negative feelings away. You will find courage to step out in full and complete faith knowing that God is with you. He wants to advance you so that you may live more abundantly.

Day Fourteen

Instant Inspiration of **Growth**

Today, I choose to feed my mind with spiritual food so that I may **grow** in Christ. I will **grow** in godliness and have the satisfaction of knowing that my life is fruitful in light of eternity. I will have the assurance of knowing that God has called and chosen me as His own. He will offer me eternal benefits.

"And the child Samuel **grew** on, and was in favor both with the Lord, and also with men." *1 Sam 2:26*

Growth

Every person should desire to grow in godliness so that they may live a fruitful life. God has given His children an opportunity to be useful and fruitful, and we should be so grateful because it takes us to the entrance into the eternal kingdom of our Lord and Savior Jesus Christ.

Love the Lord with all your heart. Tell God everyday that you love Him. Be intimate with and increase your love for Him and expect God to start increasing you in every area of your life. The nearer you draw to Him, the more He grows in you. As you grow in Him your faith will be strengthened and you will enjoy the satisfaction of knowing that your life is fruitful in light of eternity.

Remember what Christ did for you. He shed His blood on the cross to purify you from your sins. He assured you that He has called and chosen you as his own. He rescued you from judgment.

God changed your heart so that you desire to know Him better. You have been safeguarded from stumbling in the sense of falling from the faith. You now stand in the presence of His glory blameless with great joy and when you step into eternity there will be a grand welcome!

Day Fifteen

Instant Inspiration of **Joy**

Today, I thank God. When I accepted His free gift of salvation, He gave me eternal **joy** that no man can give nor take away. I am **joyful** because although I have sinned, I have not forfeited my right to eternal life. He has been faithful and just to cleanse me from all unrighteousness. I have **joy** down in my soul.

"Consider it pure **joy**, my brothers and sisters, whenever you face trials of many kinds, because you know that the testing of your faith produces perseverance." *James 1:2-3*

Joy

JOY! You should have joy way down in your soul. When you go before God with clean hands and a pure heart, He rewards you with joy and entry into His presence. *Make a joyful noise unto the Lord!*

Joy is a protection and a strength. It is a reward to the overcomer of fear, depression and all manners of sin. Joy insulates us from the cares of the world.

As you walk in a state of perpetual joy and victory, your journey seems shorter and your load feels lighter. Be determined to experience the joy of the Lord in your life.

Ask God to fill you with joy. Tell satan that you will not be weak and you will not break. Move in the direction that is pleasing to God. Radiate joy that is infectious in nature and draws others to a saving knowledge of Christ.

With joy, you enjoy the benefits of peace and happiness that no one can take away. You deserve it and you are worth it. It is beneficial, healthy, and correct to seek after joy. God desires us to have eternal joy. Exercise strength and bask in divine healing in every area of your life through the joy of the Lord.

Day Sixteen

Instant Inspiration of **Positive Thinking**

Today, I will **think positive**, even if I am not feeling very **positive**. God has helped me to discipline my thoughts and guided me in truth. I have been transformed by the renewing of my mind. I am in God's will and living free.

"Do not conform to the pattern of this world, but be transformed by the renewing of your mind. Then you will be able to test and approve what God's will is—his good, pleasing and perfect will." *Romans 12:2*

Positive Thinking

Negative thoughts come to every person. You cannot stop them from coming but you can govern your negative thought life by not speaking it. The less you speak negative the less you will think negative. Don't continue to allow negativity to delay what God wants to release to you.

Sometimes, we go through the trials and tribulations of life and invite mediocrity and defeat into our lives through our negative thoughts and speaking. The little ANTS (Automatic Negative Thoughts) keep crawling all around us but you must step on them. Tell them that you don't know how they got into this world but they are going to get out of yours.

Change the invitation. Start inviting good thoughts into your mind. Tell yourself, *"I can do all things through Christ."* When you change the invitation you are inviting God's blessings into your life.

It's impossible to think defeat and expect victory. How can God's promises come to pass if you don't believe them? The good news is that the promises are still in your future. God did not cancel them because you were negative. Believe in His promises and know that He still has the answer you need and is working things in your favor.

When you refuse to think or speak negative, those ANTS will die stillborn. It will never become reality. Get into agreement with God think positive!

Day Seventeen

Instant Inspiration of **Patience**

Today, I will be **patient** and of good courage even if my rights are violated. My patience reveals my faith in God and I will no longer be in bondage to a natural response when things go wrong. Instead, I have the Lord's strength to respond with patience and in complete trust in the Father's power and purpose.

"Be still before the LORD and wait **patiently** for him; do not fret when men succeed in their ways, when they carry out their wicked schemes." *Psalm 37:7*

Patience

Many people face challenges with being patient on a day to day basis. When all is well, patience is easy to demonstrate. When we are faced with challenges and struggles our patience is very limited. So often, we don't realize that patience is a weak point that we must constantly work to improve.

Times are really tough and so many people have become discouraged. Some have been asking and praying to God but feel as if He is taking too long. So they start worrying and allowing their minds to race, trying to find their own solution to a problem that only —HE— can fix. Humble yourself and stop worrying. The proud man is full of himself, while the humble man is full of God. The proud man worries; the humble man waits. We must learn to seek God's face and not His hand.

Keep in mind that satan's plan is to keep you in a state of frustration. Although patience may be your weak point, it's satan's strong point. He will invest any amount of time to defeat you. That's why you can't be so quick to get upset or angered.

It's much better to be patient than to be proud, if you want to inherit God's promises. When things don't go our way or don't happen as quickly as you would like them to, you must continue to do good and rejoice in hope while we wait. If you can just endure and be patient the bible says, "The Lord shall renew our strength and we shall mount up with wings like eagles."

Day Eighteen

Instant Inspiration of **Wisdom**

Today, I ask that God will increase my **wisdom**. If He grants me **wisdom**, I will be able to see things from His perspective and respond according to scriptural principles. **Wisdom** will give me strength, understanding, direction, and favor before God and man.

"Do not forsake **wisdom**, and she will protect you; love her, and she will watch over you. **Wisdom** is supreme; therefore get **wisdom**. Though it cost all you have, get understanding."

Proverbs 4:6-7

Wisdom

Do you want to be wise? Would you like to have the ability to make better choices by using good, sound judgment? If so, ask God to grant you wisdom. He already knows exactly what you need but wants you to ask.

Wisdom give you confidence, strength, and vision. Wisdom makes you trust, obey, and acknowledge God. We should really focus on being a person with great wisdom because it's an invaluable gift from God and one of the most important virtues in life. Knowing that wisdom is available to us, why not gain wisdom through the Word of God.

Sometimes we have knowledge but don't have wisdom. Having knowledge, information and facts is always great but ask God for wisdom as well. Wisdom will show you how and when to apply or put it all together. For example: Knowledge is knowing how to manage your money, budgeting, spending, and saving. Wisdom is understanding how money impacts the quality of your life and future.

Don't be interested in the wisdom of the world but the wisdom of God. Being guided by His wisdom always end with great results. Walk in wisdom and live in truth. Trust that God will give you the ability to see matters as He sees them in order to judge them correctly. Decree and declare that *wisdom will help build your house!*

Day Nineteen

Instant Inspiration of **Forgiveness**

Today, I choose to **forgive** and let go of any anger that I may be harboring inside of me. Instead of seeking revenge on people who have hurt me, I will pray for them. I choose to let go and be at peace, while allowing God to deal with him or her as He, in His perfect wisdom sees fit.

"For if you **forgive** other people when they sin against you, your heavenly Father will also **forgive** you. 15 But if you do not **forgive** others their sins, your Father will not **forgive** your sins."
Matthew 6:14-15

Forgiveness

Think of how many times have you made mistakes or even used bad judgment. How many times afterward have you thought to yourself, "Maybe I should have made a better choice?" You were hoping and praying for forgiveness. Probably countless times, if you are honest enough to recognize that you are not a perfect person.

The bible says, that it is God's desire that we are kind and forgiving of one another. Even if it's a person who has caused you much grief and pain. You must forgive them. It doesn't mean that you are opening a door for the hurt or abuse to continue. It means that you are honoring God's commands so that you may experience less emotional pain and improved health.

Just as God forgives you, He wants you to let go of any bitterness and anger toward any other person and forgive them as well. He wants you to have healthy thinking and feelings so that you can live a healthy life. Satan wants you to be resentful and unforgiving so that he won't have to attack but you attack yourself. Refuse to let the enemy control your emotions and thinking because he will then control your mind.

Don't feel like you are inviting further injury. The truth is that you are inviting forgiveness to lead you down the path of healing and peace.

Day Twenty

Instant Inspiration of **Knowledge**

Today, I will seek to acquire more **knowledge**. God gives me **knowledge** to protect myself from the difficulties of life and to allow love to express itself in good works. I also understand that more **knowledge** I have, the easier it will be for me to learn and the smarter I will become.

"The heart of the discerning acquires **knowledge**, for the ears of the wise seek it out." *Proverbs 18:15*

Knowledge

Having knowledge of God and His Word is one of the most valuable benefits. The bible says, "My people are destroyed from lack of knowledge" (Hosea 4:6).

Knowing God and His Word helps one to know how to think about God. It separates you from the pollutions of the world.

How would you feel about being presented to God without a spot, wrinkle, or blemish? That is how we should be presented, if we want to reach heaven. We must keep ourselves unspotted from the world and increase our spiritual knowledge of the Lord, His Son Jesus Christ, His Holy Spirit, and all of their ways. The reason for this is that God wants sanctification and transformation to take place in our lives.

Aren't you interested in knowing what God is doing and exactly why He is doing it? God loves to transmit knowledge to His children but many of us have never been taught how to hear from Him. You must desire and be willing to personally seek Him and He will give it to you.

Ask God to give you knowledge. Seek and knock, and he will guide your thoughts. If you are open to receiving supernatural communication from God, The Holy Spirit can and will communicate to you. You can literally pull knowledge directly from the Lord and He wants you to have it.

Day Twenty-One

Instant Inspiration of Destiny:

Today, I will walk in my **destiny**. God has already provided provision for the vision and it will surely come at His appointed time. He will fulfill His purpose for me and I shall accomplish that which I please and it shall prosper.

"For I know the plans I have for you," declares the Lord, "plans to prosper you and not to harm you, plans to give you hope and a future." *Jeremiah 29:11*

Destiny

Every person here on earth has a divine destiny that Almighty God desires us to fulfill. Sometimes we doubt it because the vision seems slow or even impossible but we must believe and it will surely come in God's appointed time.

Fulfilling your destiny is important because there are people here on earth who will never know God unless they see and get to know Him through you. You are divinely destined to do an even greater work than Jesus did. Ephesians 2:10 says, "For we are his workmanship, created in Christ Jesus for good works, which God prepared beforehand, that we should walk in them." God has already equipped you, so don't doubt it.

You were predestined to be like Jesus and God already knew before your were born what He wants you to fulfill here on earth. He knew you when you were just an image on the inside of Him. You have been divinely equipped with the power to reveal Jesus in your life.

God wants to build you up so that you may receive His inheritance. You are uniquely and specially made. The Lord is going to fulfill His purpose for you. For He already knows the plans that He has for you. The bible says, "He shall perfect and complete you and you shall lack in nothing."

Day Twenty-Two

Instant Inspiration of **Understanding**

Today, I ask God for **understanding** of the things that are freely given to me by Him. I call out for insight on of the things that cause me to be confused. I ask that I am lightened in my **understanding** so that I may consistently seek after God.

"Trust in the Lord with all your heart and lean not on your own **understanding**;"

"Do not be wise in your own eyes; fear the Lord and shun evil." *Proverbs 3:5&7*

Understanding

Sometimes things are beyond your understanding. Especially when you feel as if you are far above your head in the daily demands of living. With bills piled high and your money running low, life can seem to be anything but easy to understand. Don't be discouraged because for everything there is a season.

Pray, ask and seek the Lord for understanding and He will give it to you. Sometimes, God reveals things in our spirits to help us understand, but our minds just don't think it's logical. Whether or not your mind and your spirit agree, you should always walk and agree in the spirit. He has called you to peace, so walk in Him.

When you feel unsure open your bible, get in the word and vision yourself understanding. See yourself ministering in the power of the Holy Spirit and let the very love of God lead you to step out in faith with hope and confidence.

In the midst of your lack of understanding and all of the daily demands of life; rise up, trust Him, and lean not to your own understanding. Expect God to grant you understanding and don't let anything stop you.

Day Twenty-Three

Instant Inspiration of Confession

Today, I boldly **confess** all of my sins and ask for forgiveness. My mind is alert, my heart is receptive, and I desire to be cleansed of all unrighteousness. If I am to serve Christ, I must **confess** and repent. God, I humbly come before you asking for your everlasting grace and mercy.

"If we **confess** our sins, he is faithful and just and will forgive us our sins and purify us from all unrighteousness."
1 John 1:9

Confession

Although confession may be hard, it's necessary. Many often feel that if they confess they will be punished. God already knows all of your sins but He is faithful and just to forgive when you confess.

We must not try and cover up or hide any of our wrongdoings from God if we want to obtain mercy from Him. Through confession and prayer, God forgives and will give you a free gift of eternal life.

Don't be ashamed or regretful of any of your transgressions. The bible says that −everyone− has sinned but if you confess, God will cleanse you from all unrighteousness. It doesn't matter if you were a fornicator, lesbian, abuser, prostitute, or murderer. God loves you.

Start confessing or speaking God's promises in faith so that you may receive them. The Lord desires to cleanse and bless you. Confess to God with great enthusiasm to be cleansed from all that would offend Him and He will give you everything you need.

God has made you more than a conqueror. Don't concern yourself with what man has to say about you. Concern yourself with what the Word of God declares as truth. Align your confession with His Word. Greater is He that is within you. The Lord is the strength of your life.

Day Twenty-Four

Instant Inspiration of **Commitment**

Today, I totally **commit** myself to God. I desire to draw near to Him so that He may draw near to me. I will honor, trust, and give thanks to the Lord. I will not serve two masters. As for me, I will serve the Lord. My will is to do His will and His will only.

"Commit to the Lord whatever you do, and he will establish your plans."
Proverbs 16:3

Commitment

Is your heart fully committed to the Lord? Do you hold fast to your faith in Christ when you are under misfortunes and trials? God wants you to stand firm and endure, even during hardships so that you may receive the crown of life that He has promised to those who love Him (James 1:12).

Many people struggle with commitment in their lives but if we could learn to truly commit our lives to Jesus, all of the other commitments in our lives will come into place. Commitment starts with loving the Lord with all of your heart, with all of your soul, and all of your mind.

Draw near to God and tell Him that you will trust and believe Him. Desire to do His will and not your own; and times of refreshing will come from the presence of the Lord. The nearer you draw to God, the nearer He will draw to you.

Choose not to doubt God and expect things to be added to you. Ask God in faith for a renewed heart and mind so that you may receive mercy and grace to help in time of need. Open the door to the Lord and He will give you what is good.

God is faithful and just and every good and perfect gift comes from Him. He is the Alpha and Omega, the Beginning and the End, the First and the Last. He is the God of your salvation. Commit yourself to Him and your goals and ideas will come to fruition.

Day Twenty-Five

Instant Inspiration of **Deliverance**

Today, I cry out to the Lord for **deliverance** from bondage and danger. I claim that God has set me free from any unclean spirits and demonic influences. All of my unwanted desires and behaviors are no longer present and my old wounds no longer hurt. Thank you Lord, "I AM FREE!"

"The righteous cry out, and the Lord hears them; he **delivers** them from all their troubles." *Psalm 34:17*

Deliverance

Life is challenging and it's the enemy's desire that you stay in bondage and danger. God will walk side by side with you through your trials. He will comfort and encourage you and He uses them to mature you in your faith.

Spiritual forces of evil come against you with flaming arrows of lust, doubt, guilt, jealousy, evil speech, and all manner of temptations. The Lord knows how to rescue and deliver you from your distress and fears.

Seek the Lord and cry out to Him in your time of trouble. Ask the Lord to deliver you and He will draw you up from the pit of destruction, while restoring everything that the enemy has ever stolen from you.

Ask god for deliverance and He can free you from destruction and wash away all of your sins. He knows all of your wrong doings and all of the plots and wrong doings against you. He will help you and redeem your life.

Speak life into your situation and tell the enemy that you will not fear or be dismayed. Stand firm, and give thanks to the Lord because His steadfast love endures forever.

The Lord is your healer, comforter, and deliverer. Glorify Him for all of the great things that He has done in your life.

Day Twenty-Six

Instant Inspiration of **Restoration**

Today, I decree and declare that my health has been **restored**. I decree and declare that my finances have been **restored**. I decree and declare that my faith has been **restored**. –EVERYTHING– that the enemy has ever stolen from me, has been **restored**!

"I will repay you for the years the locusts have eaten— the great locust and the young locust, the other locusts and the locust swarm— my great army that I sent among you. You will have plenty to eat, until you are full, and you will praise the name of the Lord your God, who has worked wonders for you; never again will my people be shamed." *Joel 2:25-26*

Restoration

Failure is painful but the evidence that God is in the restoration business is astonishing. He will reclaim and restore those who are eternally His, by releasing them from bondage.

Often we make promises to make amends with God because of our past sin and indiscretions but God says we have it all wrong. One of His most incredible promises is that He will make up for our destroyed years.

All of the years that have been wasted, stripped , and broken by the enemy shall be restored. The losses that you and your family have experienced will be returned to it's original condition and there is no way to repay Him.

His plan for you may have been interrupted because of the sin that you allowed to enter into your life. Your soul may feel beaten, broken, and hopeless but don't condemn yourself. Forgive and pray for yourself and others as well. God is going to start you all over again, and fill your life with His precious blessings.

It may take time to recover but God is faithful. Don't grow fearful and anxious as you wait for things to get better. Patiently waiting is a part of the process. Often, the second journey in God's will for a person's life is far greater than the original. Submit yourself to Him.

Day Twenty-Seven

Instant Inspiration of **Healing**

Today, I ask for Gods **healing** for every disease and every affliction. I will be in good health and it will go well with my soul. I will resist the devil and go to God, and He will give me rest. For God's power is made perfect in my weakness.

"The Lord will keep you free from every disease. He will not inflict on you the horrible diseases you knew in Egypt, but he will inflict them on all who hate you." *Deuteronomy 7:15*

Healing

Are you asking and praying to God for healing? Are you feeling like the ability to get well is so far-fetched, regardless of what you do? When Jesus shed His blood on the cross for our salvation from sin, He also bore the stripes on His body for our healing from sickness.

God wants you to be whole. He wants you to be whole in your spirit, soul, and body. Satan tries to discourage and defeat you by telling you that you are getting worse and can't be healed. Do not lend an ear to the enemy and allow him to shake your faith because your faith can make you well.

God desires for you to be in good health and will heal all of your diseases but He wants you to hold on to your faith. Through your faith, He can move mountains and heal all who are oppressed by the devil.

Get in right standing with God and secure your relationship with Him to remain being healthy and avoid being rebellious. Rebellion toward Him only causes the same condition to occur in our spiritual lives. Spiritual cancer will eat away your life. God wants you to be spiritually and physically healthy. He will give you victory through our Lord Jesus Christ.

Day Twenty-Eight

Instant Inspiration of **Worship**

Today, I will **worship** the Lord. "Bless the Lord, O my soul." For it is He that forgives all of my iniquity, heals all my diseases, redeems my life from the pit, and crowns me with steadfast love and mercy. "I will **worship** my Father in spirit and in truth!"

"Do not forget the covenant I have made with you, and do not **worship** other gods. Rather, **worship** the Lord your God; it is he who will deliver you from the hand of all your enemies."
2Kings 17:38-39

Worship

We are to worship God to glorify, honor, praise, exalt, and please Him. Worship time is a time when we pay deep, sincere, awesome respect, love, and fear to the One who created us. He is the one who holds our eternal destiny in His hands.

Your worship not only honors and magnifies God but it is also for your own edification and strength. Worship will help you prepare for eternal life in heaven with God and Christ. You are to worship God because He is God.

Your extravagant love and extreme submission to the Holy One flows out of the reality that God loved you first and He is worthy to be praised. Even when God's help and blessings are not evident in your life, you should still worship Him.

When you honor and worship God, He will commune with you. When you offer God your true worship you are inviting Him to inspect your heart for anything that is not like Him and to transform you into His likeness. His love is steadfast and the bible says, "He will rejoice over you with gladness."

Rejoice and praise His name. Bless and give great thanks to the Lord at all times.

Day Twenty-Nine

Instant Inspiration of **Adoration**

Today, **adoration** is my focus. I will personally connect with my Savior, who showers me with His patient love. I desire to grow in holiness and will exalt the Lord as head above all.

"Yours, Lord, is the greatness and the power and the glory and the majesty and the splendor, for everything in heaven and earth is yours. Yours, Lord, is the kingdom; you are exalted as head over all. Wealth and honor come from you; you are the ruler of all things. In your hands are strength and power to exalt and give strength to all. Now, our God, we give you thanks, and praise your glorious name." *1 Chronicles 29:11-13*

Adoration

Exalt the Lord as Head above all because every great thing comes through Him. He upholds the universe and is the truth and the life. God has been so good to you and He deserves your deepest love and respect on a daily basis.

Live a life of overflowing praise. Adore Him and it will produce significant benefits in your walk with Him. It is God's desire that you commit to Him. Ask Him for His grace and power to help you. Begin to saturate yourself with God's Word because it will fuel a lifestyle of adoration.

The more knowledge you have of God, the more in depth and intimate your praise to Him will be. Plead with Him to teach you how to honor and exalt Him with praise. Adore God for every truth that you learn about Him.

When you adore God, you are realizing whose presence you are entering because your focus will be on Him. As you enter His presence in adoration, you will find your faith being strengthened and the power of God will begin to manifest in your life.

God is mighty and you need Him for everything and every moment of your life. By His grace, you have been saved.

Day Thirty

Instant Inspiration of **Praise**

Today, **praise** shall continually be on my lips. Regardless of my circumstances, I believe that my **praise** will change the atmosphere. My **praise** is my highest calling and I believe that the peace of God will keep my heart and mind. My **praise** is my strength and I shall be blessed and prosper.

"**Praise** the Lord, all you nations; extol him, all you peoples. For great is his love toward us, and the faithfulness of the Lord endures forever. **Praise** the Lord." *Psalm 117:1-2*

Praise

Even in your darkest hour you should praise God and remain joyful, regardless of what is happening in your life. We are not to become bitter over life's circumstances but rather to continue to rejoice in the Lord. The devil will try and send you evil and blame it on God but if you resist him, he will flee from you.

Bless the Lord, bless His Holy name! For He is our refuge and fortress in times of trouble. God will never fail or desert you in the midst of your trials. With an attitude of praise, lift your voice to the Lord. Tell Him that you will submit to Him and never deny Him no matter what happens.

Boast in the Lord, even when all looks bleak. Don't look at a situation through your natural eyes but through the eyes of faith and believe that He is going to send you an answer. Press on into the spirit so that you sense a real joy, and praise comes forth because you have so much to praise Him for.

Praising God when you are feeling sick, depressed, lonely, weary –or any other feeling of pain–will bring liberation and healing. Praising the Lord can bring quick relief from despondence and oppression. Develop a vocabulary of praise and the Lord will lift your soul and keep you alive. Praise the Lord, for His mercy endureth forever!

Day Thirty-One

Instant Inspiration of **Believe**

Today, I **believe** in God. He has forgiven my sins and I have peace with God. He has redeemed my life from destruction by giving His one and only son to die on the cross for me; to take my punishment that I deserve for the sin in my life. I **believe** in the Lord Jesus!

"Therefore I tell you, whatever you ask for in prayer, believe that you have received it, and it will be yours."
Mark11:24

Believe

We often go through trials and difficulties that fill us with unbelief. The bible says that *"The Lord is our strength and our shield."* Sometimes we just have to slow down and wait on Him so that we are reminded of our complete and utter dependence on His strength.

Your strength will never measure up to God's strength; so give Him all of your worries, headaches, and heartaches. Take those old wounds and believe God's Word. Stand on His promises and press on confidently in joy because He is your hope and your future.

Listen to God's voice and believe His wondrous ability to bless your life. He said in His Word that if you believe Him, you have the right to become His child and that He rewards those who seek Him.

Don't be deceived by the tricks of the enemy because it is his desire that you stay in a miry bog. Refuse to continue to allow your own misguided beliefs to tear you down.

Don't keep stumbling through the pieces that have become the rubble of destruction in your life. You have been justified by faith and set free in Christ Jesus from the law of sin and death. "BELIEVE GOD!"

If you would like to write in reference to this book, request more copies, or contact the author please feel free to do so at:

Andrea Freeman
P.O. Box 18151
Baltimore, MD 21220

andreasbook@classy5.com

Also available for purchase by the author:

"No Barriers, No Limits!"

"Think Up, And Go Up!"

www.ingramcontent.com/pod-product-compliance
Lightning Source LLC
LaVergne TN
LVHW051133080426
835510LV00018B/2390